Green Turtle R

Written by Linda Johns

Illustrated by Richard Moore

My family went to Grandpa's
house for Thanksgiving.
We did something better
than eat turkey.

2

We looked for green turtles with Turtle Experience! Turtle Experience is a group of people who save green turtles.

4

Grandpa lives on Long Island
in New York.
"Green turtles like Long Island
in the summer," Grandpa said.
"When it starts to get cold,
most turtles swim to warmer water,
but a few stay behind."

"It's too cold for them here now,"
Grandpa said.
"They get so cold that
they can't move."

6

I was cold too.
"The turtles must be
really cold," I said.

"We need to find them
and get them help,"
Grandpa said.

Grandpa and I walked on the beach with other people from the group.

"Marissa, look!" Grandpa said.
There was a turtle far ahead
of us.

9

We hurried to the turtle.
"Should we put him
in a blanket?" I asked.

10

"No," Grandpa said.
"Turtles can die
if they warm up too fast.
It's best to let the vet warm up
the turtle."

I patted the turtle's back.
"You'll be okay, Chilly," I said.

Grandpa laughed.
"That's a good name,"
he said.

We gave Chilly
to the vet.

"Thank you so much
for finding this turtle," she said.
"It wouldn't live through the night
on the beach."

13

At Grandpa's house,
Mom and Dad gave us
hot chocolate.
I told them all about Chilly.

"If all goes well,
Chilly can return to the sea
in the summer," Grandpa said.

I hoped I could come back
to see that.

The next summer, Turtle Experience
sent 16 green turtles back
to the sea.
Grandpa and I waved good-bye
as Chilly hurried home
to the ocean.